ANIMALS GROWING UP™

HOW PENGUINS GROW UP

Lisa Idzikowski

Enslow Publishing
101 W. 23rd Street
Suite 240
New York, NY 10011
USA

enslow.com

WORDS TO KNOW

chick A baby penguin.

down Fluffy fuzz covering baby birds.

flippers A penguin's wings.

habitat A place where animals live and grow.

incubate To keep an egg warm until it hatches.

krill A small shrimp-like animal.

predator An animal that kills other animals for food.

species A group of living things that are alike and have the same scientific name.

CONTENTS

BABY PENGUINS

Fuzzy baby penguins look so soft. Their fluffy, plump bodies are covered with down. Wild penguins live in the Southern Hemisphere, from near the equator to as far south as Antarctica.

An emperor penguin chick has light gray down on its body.

FAST FACT

Baby penguins are called chicks.

HABITATS

Penguins live in many different habitats. Some live in icy cold lands or on warm islands. Some live in cool forests or near deserts. Penguins are seabirds and are never far from the ocean.

FAST FACT

Penguins spend about three-quarters of their time in the water, but they raise chicks on land.

African penguin chicks live in warm weather in southern Africa.

SO MANY KINDS

Most scientists say that there are seventeen or eighteen different species of penguins. The emperor penguin is the largest. The little penguin is the smallest.

The little penguin is sometimes called the little blue penguin because of its bluish color.

A little penguin chick has brown down, but it will grow blue feathers.

PENGUINS ARE BIRDS

Penguins are birds. They have feathers and their babies hatch from eggs. But unlike other birds, penguins have solid, heavy bones. Instead of flying, they swim in the sea.

A penguin uses its flippers to glide through water.

FAST FACT

A penguin's wings are called flippers.

PART OF A COLONY

When it's time to nest, penguins come to land. Most species form nesting groups, or colonies, to find a mate and to pick a nesting spot.

FAST FACT

Some penguin colonies have thousands of pairs of nesting penguins.

Gentoo penguins live in colonies in the Falkland Islands in the South Atlantic Ocean.

13

AT THE NEST

Some penguins build nests as stone or grass filled dents in the ground. Others even dig holes or burrows! After a mother penguin lays an egg or two, both parents take turns incubating and guarding the eggs.

Rockhopper penguins watch over their egg.

FAST FACT

Galapagos penguins sometimes nest in the cracks of lava.

WHERE ARE YOU?

Penguin colonies are noisy. How do penguin parents find their hungry chicks? Squeaks and squawks tell a parent penguin, "I'm here, and I'm hungry!"

FAST FACT

Penguin parents will only take care of their own chicks.

A hungry gentoo penguin calls out for its mother.

HUNGRY PENGUINS

Penguins hunt for food in the sea. They gobble up small fish, squid, and krill. Emperor penguins eat up to about 13 pounds (6 kilograms) a day. That's a lot of seafood!

FAST FACT

Penguin parents spit up mashed fish and feed it to their hungry chicks.

An emperor penguin feeds her chick mushy fish she has coughed up from her stomach.

19

GUARD THOSE CHICKS!

Penguin parents keep watch over their chicks. While one parent is away feeding, the other stands guard. Chicks must be kept safe from the cold and predators.

The guard stage for many penguins lasts about two to three weeks.

A Magellanic penguin guards its chicks from danger.

GROW, GET FAT, AND LEAVE

Penguin chicks grow and get fat. Baby down is pushed out by growing feathers. The chicks march down to the sea, splash off with the other young penguins, and leave their parents.

FAST FACT

The age a young penguin leaves the nest depends on what species it is. Adélie penguin chicks leave at 7 to 9 weeks. King penguin chicks leave at 13 months.

Adélie penguins leave their nests and jump into the sea.

LEARN MORE

Books

Bedoyere, Camilla de la. *The Wild Life of Penguins*. New York, NY: Windmill Books, 2015.

Hall, Margaret. *Penguins and Their Chicks*. North Mankato, MN: Capstone Press, 2018.

Richmond, Ben. *Baby Penguin's First Waddles*. New York, NY: Sterling Children's Books, 2018.

Websites

National Geographic Kids: Emperor Penguin
kids.nationalgeographic.com/animals/emperor-penguin/#emperor-penguin-group-snow.jpg
Learn all about emperor penguins.

San Diego Zoo Kids: African Penguin
kids.sandiegozoo.org/animals/african-penguin
Read fun facts about African penguins.

INDEX

Published in 2019 by Enslow Publishing, LLC.
101 W. 23rd Street, Suite 240, New York, NY 10011

Copyright © 2019 by Enslow Publishing, LLC.

Library of Congress Cataloging-in-Publication Data
Names: Idzikowski, Lisa, author.
Title: How penguins grow up / Lisa Idzikowski.
Description: New York, NY : Enslow Publishing, 2019. | Series: Animals growing up | Includes bibliographical references and index. | Audience: Grades K to 3.
Identifiers: LCCN 2017046600| ISBN 9780766096592 (library bound) | ISBN 9780766096608 (pbk.) | ISBN 9780766096615 (6 pack)
Subjects: LCSH: Penguins—Juvenile literature. | Penguins—Infancy—Juvenile literature.
Classification: LCC QL696.S473 I39 2017 | DDC 598.4713/92—dc23
LC record available at https://lccn.loc.gov/2017046600

Printed in the United States of America

To Our Readers: We have done our best to make sure all website addresses in this book were active and appropriate when we went to press. However, the author and the publisher have no control over and assume no liability for the material available on those websites or on any websites they may link to. Any comments or suggestions can be sent by email to customerservice@enslow.com.

Photos Credits: Cover, p. 1 Steve Bloom/Barcroft Media/Getty Images; pp. 4–23 (background image), 15, 23 (main photos) Chip Somodevilla/Getty Images; pp. 5, 7, 19 Foreverhappy/Shutterstock.com; p. 9 China Photos/Getty Images; p. 11 dangdumrong/Shutterstock.com; p. 13 Mitsuaki Iwago/Minden Pictures/Getty Images; p. 17 Keren Su/China Span/Getty Images; p. 21 Steve Bloom Images/Alamy Stock Photo.